Copyright 2013 by Tandy Ruoff and Sam Smith

All rights reserved. This book is protected by the copyright laws of the United Kingdom. This book may not be copied or reprinted for comercial gain or profit. We have used different Bible translations so that each scriputre that has been used is as clear and simple for the children to apply to their lives.
Scripture quotations are taken from:

The New English Bible, copyright © Cambridge University Press and Oxford University Press 1961, 1970. All rights reserved.

The Common English Bible®, CEB® Copyright © 2010, 2011 by Common English Bible.™ Used by permission. All rights reserved worldwide.

Scripture quotations marked (NLT) are taken from the Holy Bible, New Living Translation, copyright © 1996, 2004, 2007 by Tyndale House Foundation. Used by permission of Tyndale House Publishers, Inc., Carol Stream, Illinois 60188. All rights reserved.

Holy Bible, New International Version®, NIV® Copyright © 1973, 1978, 1984, 2011 by Biblica, Inc.®Used by permission. All rights reserved worldwide.

Scripture is taken from GOD'S WORD®, © 1995 God's Word to the Nations. Used by permission of Baker Publishing Group.

ISBN-13: 978-1494945381

ISBN-10: 149494538X

Special assistance: Philippa-Jo Dobson and Katherine McAllen

Design and Artwork: Kimlyn Harbottle

© Tandy Ruoff / Sam Smith

Encountering God with our senses

© Tandy Ruoff / Sam Smith

CONTENTS

Endorsements	Page 6
Foreword	Page 7
Introduction	Page 9
1: Touch	Page 15
2: Hearing	Page 25
3: Sight	Page 35
4: Taste	Page 45
5: Smell	Page 53
Testimonies	Page 61
Questions and Answers	Page 63
About The Authors	Page 67

Endorsements

"What a blessing and joy to have such valuable materials to use to impart to our children the love, goodness and true nature of God, through our five senses. These materials are well done, easy to use and readily received and understood by the children. Thank you Tandy and Sam for your hard work, love and dedication... not only to your own beautiful children, but to those around the world. You have made the lessons fun and profound! I have personally used these materials and highly recommend them for bringing children into a closer relationship to their heavenly Father... Papa God. He is a loving creator who has formed each child from before the foundations of the world. Let's help them learn more about Him through the very senses He designed in each and every one. Again, thank you for pursuing after God and bringing the children along."

Marilyn Seth

Children's Minister and Pre School Director

"Tandy and Sam came to our Church weekend away and led our children into new encounters with God using their material, "Encountering God with our senses". It began a journey for our children and for us as leaders to expect and experience the MORE of God. This journey is an adventure and is full of WOW moments where our children are learning their true identity as Sons and Daughters of Father God and how He fully speaks to them."

Steph Cox

Senior Leader Christ Church Peckham

"A truly remarkable and powerful tool in training children and developing a deep and real relationship with Jesus. I am so impressed and blessed by all I read! Detailed and yet so easy to follow, you can feel the way the Holy Spirit can use this tool to minister to children. *Encountering God with your senses* is a unique and profound journey for children to develop an understanding of how to have a real and lasting relationship with God. A great book for children's ministries and parents alike."

Helen Healy
Primary School Head Teacher

"Children love to be taught Bible stories, but more than that, they love to know and encounter God for themselves. It is in the encounter that children come alive to God. This material is excellent at facilitating that encounter. We have used it on our Church Weekend and the children loved it. Every church and children's ministry should use Encountering God with our Senses as an insightful, Biblical and simple way to help our amazing children experience God in a fresh way."

Revd Malcolm Macdonald,
Vicar of St Mary's Loughton, Essex

This is a refreshing multi sensory resource! So simple, like it should be. An awesome way of releasing your children's potential, actively encouraging them to encounter Jesus. This program will produce thousands upon thousands of stories of children experiencing God, through the power of the Holy Spirit.

Pete Oakley
Co-founder and director of Pulse Children's and Youth Ministries

Foreword

Are you ready for some new and fresh material to teach in your Sunday school group?
Are you ready for your children to meet with their *living* and *loving* heavenly Father?
Are you ready to be amazed at how children can so easily encounter Father God and receive from him?

We have written this programme because our heart is for children to encounter and experience Father God through an intimate relationship with Him. We want to equip children to recognize Gods presence, to expect Him to reveal Himself in different ways and help children to really *know* Him. We would call this intimacy, for the children we would call it being "super close" to their Father God. *

We believe that this teaching is on Father God's agenda as children have a very special place in His heart and He has plans to use them to reveal His glory to the world. Children can push boundaries and open doors because of their innocence and boldness, so we need to equip our children with tools to do this. We are hungry to see the supernatural in their lives when it comes from a place of intimacy with Father God.

We really encourage you to ask Father God to bring you personal revelation of this teaching, before you teach it to the children. When we have that, we can lead the children not just with head knowledge but also with heart experience. This then opens a door for them, which they can run through into amazing encounters with Father God.

It's important that you ask Father God what is on His heart for the children in *your* group. We are all on a journey with Him and at different places, so different parts of this teaching may need to be adapted or emphasised depending on the needs of your group.

Please remember, as with any teaching, that it is the Holy Spirit who will bring revelation to the children's hearts. Please don't be discouraged if you don't "see" what you'd hoped for happening with the children. It may take some children a few weeks to "tune in" but also be prepared for Father God to move amazingly! Believe that the Holy Spirit is working and let

Father God lead you step by step. Pray for the gift of discernment and be ready to adapt your plans as the Holy Spirit leads. Above all else have fun with Father God!

Tandy Ruoff and Sam Smith

*In Gen 4.1 it says Adam *knew* Eve, in John 17.3 Jesus says "this is eternal life that they *know* you." And in Exodus 33.13 Moses asks God that he may *know* Him. All these *"knows"* have the same root meaning in Hebrew of "Yada" meaning "close intimacy."

Introduction

What we have given you here is a very concentrated plan of teaching. You can take this teaching and stretch and adapt it to fit your group's needs and timetable. The teaching works really well as part of a holiday club where you may have more time to focus on each lesson. If you are using the "Encountering God with your senses" on a Sunday morning you may need to adjust the programme. Our experience is that each part takes about thirty minutes. The suggested age group for this teaching is Primary age (5-11 year olds). However this is flexible, both older and younger children have accessed this teaching in the past.

We have separated the teaching into two parts. Each lesson follows the same plan:

1st Part:

Aim: to wake up each sense!

- Focus
- Worship
- Mr Spuddy drama
- Bible story
- Drama from Bible story
- Teaching
- Craft and Games

The first part can go in a different order but we suggest you finish with the teaching.

2nd Part:

Aim: For God to encounter children through each sense

- Encounter time
- Journaling
- Heart 2 Heart
- Prayer
- Testimonies

1st Part:

Focus

At the start of every sense we have highlighted the focus of that particular lesson. Take time to hear what the Holy Spirit wants to highlight for your specific group.

Worship

Worship is very important for many reasons. Worship will help to focus the children on Father God. Worship will bring you all onto the presence of Father God and set the tone for the morning. Of course use praise & action songs but also try to have worship songs where children can express themselves freely. If you are short of time even one song would be great.

Mr Spuddy drama

This as a fun, relaxed short drama to emphasise how the whole of the body is important. Mr Spuddy is either a man dressed up or is just a drawn potato head or the actual toy or even get a potato head puppet!

Bible teaching

We look at the Word and use a Bible story to start thinking about each sense and how it was used in the story. We have often added a time for the children to act out the Bible story so that we are creating an opportunity for all children to learn and understand through different learning styles.

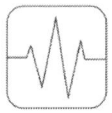

Life Application

This is where we talk with the children about how the teaching is relevant to them and how it can change us. This brings the first part all together and sets the scene for encounter time.

Games & craft

This can be used to again emphasise the teaching in many ways. It can be used as a break in the first part as the children have been listening hard! The craft and games are at the end of the lesson so you can decide where in the lesson to place them. We suggest games in the lesson to help give the children a chance to stretch their legs and can be used as a tool to compliment the teaching. The craft can be at the end to bring the lesson to a conclusion. Or it can go where you feel fits your group best.

© Tandy Ruoff / Sam Smith

2nd Part:

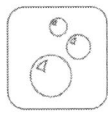

Encounter/Soaking Time

Each child will need a journal or notebook for this time. Soaking time is a chance for the children to encounter Father God. Encourage children to find their own space and try to be still so they don't disturb others. Encourage children that Father God will show himself to them, and that He has lots of different ways to do that. There is no wrong way, every way Father God talks to us is good.

We have given you a focus for each time. After a few minutes give children the option to start drawing or writing in their books what Father God has shown them.

Heart 2 Heart

This is where we give room for the children to share what Father God has shown them in a small group setting. The adult can then help the children see where they can apply that to their lives and take it out to others. Encourage your small group leaders to pray with children or talk to children as needed.

Prayer

Prayer is essential throughout the programme but allowing the children to pray with you and by themselves will further develop their relationship with Father God.

© Tandy Ruoff / Sam Smith

Lesson 1

Touch

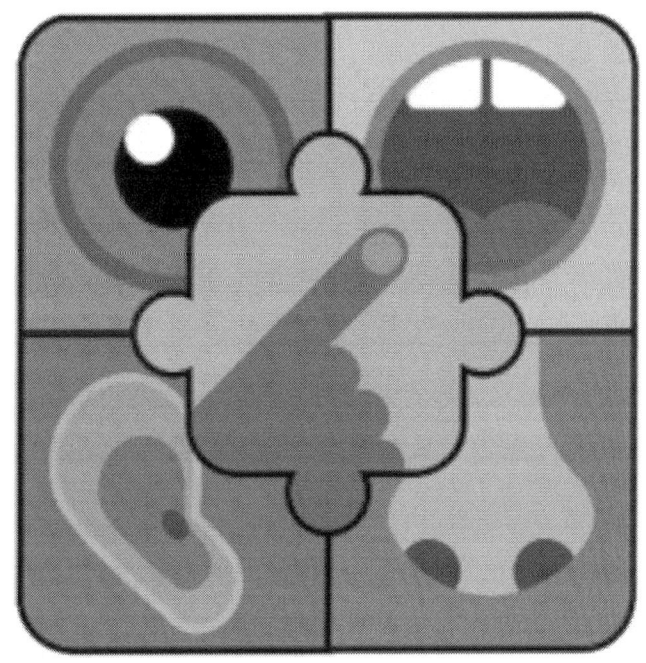

© Tandy Ruoff / Sam Smith

Touch

 ## Focus

"Jesus wants each of us to have an encounter and to meet with our heavenly Father God in a real and tangible way. We know that Father God is always with us but He desires special time with us so we can experience Him through His touch on our lives, these times are called an encounter."

 ## Worship

Spend some time now or at another point before Encounter Time worshipping Father God with the children. Worship will bring you all into the presence of Father God and set the tone/atmosphere for the session.

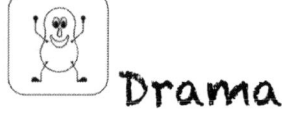 # Drama

"Mr Spuddy and touch."

> ### Scripture for Drama: 1 Corinthians 12:21-27 (CEB)
>
> So the eye can't say to the hand, "I don't need you," or in turn, the head can't say to the feet, "I don't need you." Instead, the parts of the body that people think are the weakest are the most necessary. The parts of the body that we think are less honourable are the ones we honour the most. The private parts of our body that aren't presentable are the ones that are given the most dignity. The parts of our body that are presentable don't need this. But God has put the body together, giving greater honour to the part with less honour so that there won't be division in the body and so the parts might have mutual concern for each other. If one part suffers, all the parts suffer with it; if one part gets the glory, all the parts celebrate with it. You are the body of Christ and parts of each other.

(Mr Spuddy is either a man dressed up or is just a drawn potato head or the actual toy or even get a potato head puppet!)

Leader: Hi everybody. Hi Mr Spuddy how are you today?

Spuddy: I am not so good!

Leader: Oh no why is that?

Spuddy: I don't like my hand!

Leader: Really *(shocked expression!)* Why is that?

Spuddy: It bugs me and its looks funny my hand looks too big for my body!

Leader: Well, your hand is really important it helps you to reach out and touch things.

Spuddy: I know, but I don't like it I can manage without it I want to pop it off!

Leader: You want to just pop it off!

Spuddy: Yeah, if I want to touch something I can use my feet or my tummy or my tongue!

Leader: Well I suppose you could but that would be kind of hard to do in some situations.

Spuddy: Maybe so but I want you to help me take it off!

Leader: Mr Spuddy can we look at a verse in the Bible?

Spuddy: Sure!

Leader: There is a verse in the Bible that is found in 1 Corinthians 12:21 and it says, *So the eye can't say to the hand, "I don't need you," or in turn, the head can't say to the feet, "I don't need you." Instead, the parts of the body that people think are the weakest are the most necessary.* Or in your case the parts that annoy you or irritate you are still important – God made them for a reason!

Spuddy: I never thought of that!

Leader: Father God gave us hands so we can touch and experience the sense of touch.

Spuddy: Can Father God touch me?

Leader: Yes He can! He can touch us with His love, His joy, His peace and we can feel the touch of His presence with us all day long.

Spuddy: Wow I think I want to keep my arm, and my hand!

Leader: I think that would be a great idea.

Spuddy: Are we going to hear the Bible story now?

Leader: We sure are, do you want to listen to it!

Spuddy: Yes please!

Bible Time

Scripture: Matthew 19:13-15 (NLT)

One day some parents brought their children to Jesus so he could lay his hands on them and pray for them. But the disciples scolded the parents for bothering him.

But Jesus said, "Let the children come to me. Don't stop them! For the Kingdom of Heaven belongs to those who are like these children." And he placed his hands on their heads and blessed them before he left.

Tell the story of when the mothers and fathers brought their children to be touched and blessed by Jesus. Explain how the disciples wouldn't let the children get close and told them off for bothering Jesus. Then share with the children Jesus' response, He stopped the disciples and allowed the children to come close to Him and how He touched and blessed them.

Allow the children to act out the story so it becomes real to them. Some of the children can be the disciples and the rest may be the parents and children. The leader can be the narrator. Describe the setting while the children act out the story.

Life Application

Ask the children how they would have felt if they had been waiting all day to see Jesus and then they weren't allowed to?

What emotions would they have felt when they finally got close to Jesus and He touched them?

Talk to the children about Jesus' touch…..

Jesus wants us to feel His presence to know His "touch" to experience Him like the children in the Bible. They got to be loved and held by Jesus, they felt His touch. He hugged and loved the children, it was a good safe place and His touch/His presence made them feel happy and good inside. He loved them.

Jesus wants us to feel His presence with us all the time. When the children had been touched by Jesus their hearts were filled with His love, His joy, His peace and they felt amazing.

Encounter/Soaking Time

- encounter through Touch

Have the children lie down all over the hall and put on worship or instrumental music. Ask the children to picture the story you have just read and ask Jesus to touch them with His love.

Pray together: (Speak this prayer slowly over children while they are resting.)

"Jesus I come close to you, thank you that it is safe, that you love me and that you are pleased to see me. Thank you that your touch is good it makes me feel loved and special."

You can also use bubbles during this time – explain to the children that you will be blowing bubbles over them, *"it is soft and gentle and it is like Jesus touching you with His presence."*

After one or two songs get the children to sit up quietly and hand out their journals and pen pots. Ask them to draw or write how they felt when Jesus touched them with His love.

Teachers Note: (You are looking for good touch words… love, joy, peaceful, warm, comforting, happy. Both a physical and an emotional experience can be had). But don't be surprised with the unexpected. We had a little girl draw a fish and said that it made her happy. We later spoke to her mum who said as a baby she was really ill and the only time she was happy was when she was in water! The way Father God touched her made her feel happy just like a fish is happy in water, she drew that in her picture – the fish represented her.

They may feel His presence all over them – they may even feel like a blanket is being wrapped around them, or they may have seen a picture or felt an emotion. Though we are dealing with touch allow all the senses to be involved in this time if that is how the child relates how they are feeling. Allow them to write if they are older.

 # HEART 2 HEART

This is where you give room for the children to share what Father God has shown them in a small group setting. The adult can then help the children see where they can apply that to their lives and take it out to others.

Talk about each child's encounter – look at each other's pictures and let them share what they felt happen to them during the soaking time. Ask the children how we can share this love with our family and friends.

 # Pray

Pray over the children to be released in touching those lives around them with the love of Jesus and remind them that Jesus loves to touch our lives in a real way so we can feel His presence.

 # Arts & crafts

Have a table with different textured materials on and allow the children to decorate, stick and write on a cut out hand. They can express themselves through art to show how they felt when Jesus touched them.

 # Games

This game would be a great game to start a session off when the children first arrive and go to their small groups.

© Tandy Ruoff / Sam Smith

Touch Bag – have a material bag with objects inside (objects the children would be able to identify through touch). The children can put one hand into the bag and feel and describe an object then guess what the object is.

You could use individual bags or boxes to put objects in to be felt. Using blindfolds makes the sense of touch more heightened.

Tag – Indoor or outdoor game where the children are allowed to run in an area and one or two children are the taggers. They can run around and tag people if a person is tagged they have to stand still until someone else who hasn't been tagged rescues them by crawling between their legs and freeing them of their "stuck" status.

© Tandy Ruoff / Sam Smith

Lesson 2

Hearing

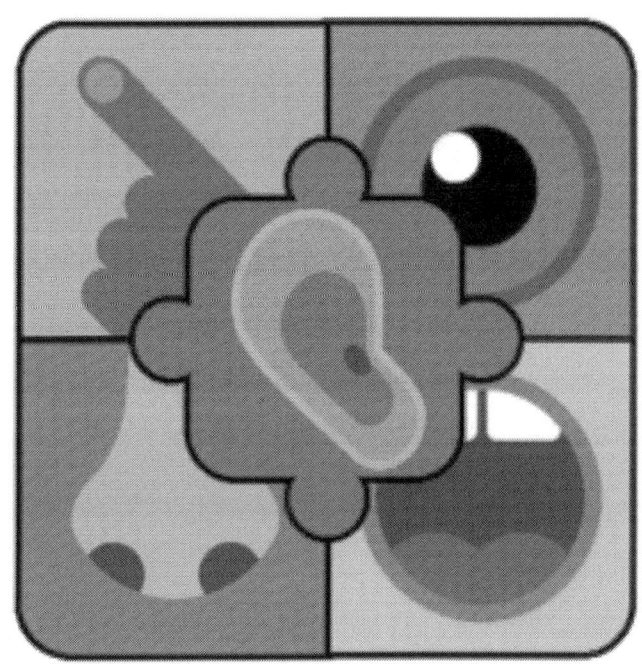

© Tandy Ruoff / Sam Smith

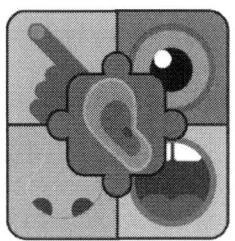

Hearing

 ### Focus

"As we learnt in our previous lesson we learnt about our sense of touch and how Father God wants to touch our lives with His presence. Today we are going to look at the sense of hearing."

 ### Worship

Spend some time now or at another point before Encounter Time worshipping Father God with the children. Worship will bring you all into the presence of Father God and set the tone/atmosphere for the session.

Drama

"Mr Spuddy and Hearing"

Leader: Hey everybody! Hi Mr Spuddy! How are you today?

Spuddy: I'm good, I just got this new hat and I am going to wear it to a party.

(Mr Spuddy tries to put the hat on but his ears are in the way so that hat doesn't fit properly!)

Leader: Your hat looks very cool Mr Spuddy.

Spuddy: No it doesn't my ears are in the way it's not supposed to sit like that!

Leader: Well why don't you go and buy a different hat Mr Spuddy maybe that one doesn't suit your head shape!

Spuddy: I want to wear this hat I am just going to pop my ears off so I can wear it!

Leader: Are you sure you want to do that?

(Mr Spuddy head pops his ears out and lays them on the floor he then puts the hat on again and it goes over his eyes.)

Leader: Oh dear Mr Spuddy now you can't hear or see! Mr Spuddy.

(Leader tries to get Mr Spuddy attention!)

(Mr Spuddy gets very frustrated and throws the cap on the floor!)

(Leader signal to Mr Spuddy to pop his ears back in!)

(Mr Spuddy puts his ears back in.)

Leader: Oh good now you can hear me! Mr Spuddy you can't pop your ears out just so you can wear a hat, look what happened when you removed your ears you couldn't hear and your hat fell over your eyes too.

Spuddy: I know, I don't know what to do!

Leader: Remember the verse we read in 1 Corinthians 12:21-22, lets read it together again, *So the eye can't say to the hand, "I don't need you," or in turn, the head can't say to the feet, "I don't need you." Instead, the parts of the body that people think are* *the weakest are the most necessary.* Or in your case the parts that annoy you or irritate you are still important – Father God made them for a reason!

Spuddy: So I can't say to my ears I don't need them is that what you are saying?

Leader: Yes that is what Father God's word is saying, He made us with eyes, ears and hands for a reason and for a purpose and we need every part of us.

Spuddy: Why do we need ears?

Leader: Why do you think we need our ears Mr Spuddy?

Spuddy: So they can hold up hats!

Leader: Well yes! But more than that, so that we can hear. We can hear our friends and teachers, mums and dads and most importantly we can hear Father God speak to us.

Spuddy: And what if your ears are blocked up like my friend Mr Courgette!

Leader: Do you mean deaf?

Spuddy: Yes!

Leader: Well Jesus healed lots of deaf people in the Bible and we can pray for healing for all our friends who have blocked up or deaf ears and Jesus can heal them.

Spuddy: Can we pray now!

Leader: Yes we can!

(Allow time for ministry if any children have problems with their hearing!)

Spuddy: I don't always hear Father God speak to me like I hear you speak to me in a loud voice!

Leader: No you are right sometimes we can't hear a loud voice but we can hear Father God's voice inside of us, the Bible calls it a still small voice!

Spuddy: I have heard a small voice inside of me especially when I am scared I hear a voice say, *"I am with you Spuddy, I never leave you!"* Is that Father God?

Leader: Yes it does sound like Father God! Do you want to hear the Bible lesson for today?

Spuddy: Yes please.

Leader: Ok let's read it!

# Bible Teaching

Read the story below out of a children's Bible. It is great fun to split the room into three groups. Allocate a group to be Samuel, Eli and Father God and have the children act out the story. Have a leader narrate the story and let the children repeat their appropriate lines.

Samuel and Eli are both sleeping… Father God calls Samuel. Get the "Samuels" to rush to the other side of the room where Eli is sleeping, they wake sleeping "Eli" up. "Eli" tells the "Samuels" to go back to bed repeat this three times. On the third time "Eli" tells "Samuel'" it is the Lord speaking to you… then Samuel goes back to bed and listen out for God to call Him again.

Scripture: 1 Samuel 3:1-21

Samuel helped Eli in the temple. His job was to keep all the lamps lit. He learned about the different types of offerings Eli made to God. Samuel also learned that praying was just like talking to God. Sometimes, though, he wondered why he did not hear God answer back.
One night Samuel was asleep when he heard a Voice calling his name, "Samuel."
"Here I am," Samuel said. He ran to Eli. "Yes, Eli. Did you call me? What did you want, sir?" Samuel asked. The old man sat up in bed and scratched his beard. "I didn't call you," he said. "Go back to sleep. It's the middle of the night."
Samuel did as he was told. No sooner was he asleep when he heard again, "Samuel!" Samuel woke up and ran to Eli.
"Yes, Eli," the boy said.
"No, my son, I didn't call you," Eli said again.
Later that night, Samuel heard for a third time the Voice saying, "Samuel! "Samuel had never heard the voice of God before. He still thought it was Eli who called him.
Once again he ran to Eli. And this time Eli knew Samuel must have heard the Lord's voice. It had been a long, long time since God had spoken to any of the people of Israel. Eli told Samuel, "The Lord God has been calling you! Answer Him next time by saying, 'Yes, Lord, I am listening.'
"The boy did as he was told. The next time the Lord spoke to Samuel, He said, "I have seen the bad things Eli's sons have been doing. From now on I will speak through you, Samuel. "The next morning Samuel told Eli everything the Lord had said. This was the first of many times God spoke to Samuel.

Life Application

Father God wants to speak to us just like He spoke to Samuel.

Ask the children the following questions to draw out of them how Father God can speak to us.

- When Father God spoke to Samuel did He shout? Or did he speak softly?
- What did Samuel have to do once Father God started to speak?
- When Father God spoke to Samuel did He wait for Samuel to be still and listen?
- What will help us to hear Father God's voice?
- Where can we be still and listen?

Father God wants to speak to us all the time about different things in our lives we have to choose to stop and to listen!

Jesus promises us that "My sheep hear my voice" – we can all hear Jesus voice! (John 10:27 NLT) It says in 1 Samuel 3:21 that …. **"He revealed himself to Samuel through his word"** *(NIV)* Revealed means once it wasn't known or was a secret but Father God showed Samuel the secrets or hidden things of His word – **the Bible.**

Father God wants us to hear His voice, audibly, in the deepest part of us and through His word. Let us encounter Father God through our hearing sense.

Story illustration: You can use this illustration to help the children understand.

When we get to a traffic light and the red man is flashing what do we do – we stop and when the green man is flashing we can go.

If a blind person gets to a traffic light how do they know when it is green or red?
When they get to the light they push the button and wait when the light goes green it goes "beep, beep, beep!" The blind person now knows it is safe to cross. They first had to stop and listen until they knew when they could go!

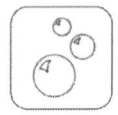

Encounter/Soaking Time

– encounter through Listening to God using our hearing sense

Have the children find a space and lie down, put on worship or instrumental music ask the children to stop and be still and listen to what Father God is saying to them.

Choose a Psalm or Scripture to read over the children. Do ask the Holy Spirit to speak to you before the lesson about which scripture would be relevant for each encounter time.

Tell the children Father God is going to speak of His love for them and as they listen to the Word of God He may speak to them through the Bible verses or He may speak to their hearts something that He wants to tell them about how much He loves them. Father God gave Samuel a message for someone else and also spoke to him about what he was going to be when he grew up. Father God can speak to us about lots of different things. As the leader see what Father God wants you to focus on in that particular lesson.

Pray together: "Thank you Father God that I can hear your voice please come and touch my life with your presence and speak to me."

After one or two songs get the children to quietly sit up and hand out their journals and pen pots. Ask them to draw or write what they heard Father God speak to them.

HEART 2 HEART

This is where you give room for the children to share what Father God has shown them in a small group setting. The adult can then help the children see where they can apply that to their lives and take it out to others.

Talk about each person's encounter – look at each other's pictures and share what each child felt happen during the soaking time. Ask the children how they can share with others about how to hear Father God.

 Pray

Pray with each child about what they heard from Father God, thanking Him that He always hears them and that we as His children can hear His voice.

Extras:

If you need extra things to do you can use the below as questions and answers in Heart to Heart groups or extended activities and ideas for further lessons:

The Bible says that *"He (God) revealed himself to Samuel through His word."*

Father God tells us good things, wonderful things about Himself in the Bible, so when we are still and read the Bible, we will hear Father God speak to us!

 Arts & crafts

Cut out a large ear for each child. Have words/letters cut out from magazines or pictures and textile fabric. Allow the children to write what they "heard" or "sensed" Father God say to them while they were soaking. Have felt tip pens or crayons available if children just want to write their own words. Cut out words which speak hope, life and encouragement.

 Games

Musical Statues (with a difference) – Play music for the children to dance around to, pause the music occasionally. When the music stops they need to stop then listen for the instruction of which shape/position they need to be in.

Talk About: We may be busy in life but when we need help or direction of what to do we need to stop and listen and Father God will speak!

Or

Sounds – Record different sounds and in the children's small groups let them listen to the sound. The children can then try and guess what the sound is and write it down. Allow the children to re-listen to the sounds and find out which ones they got right.

Lesson 3

Seeing

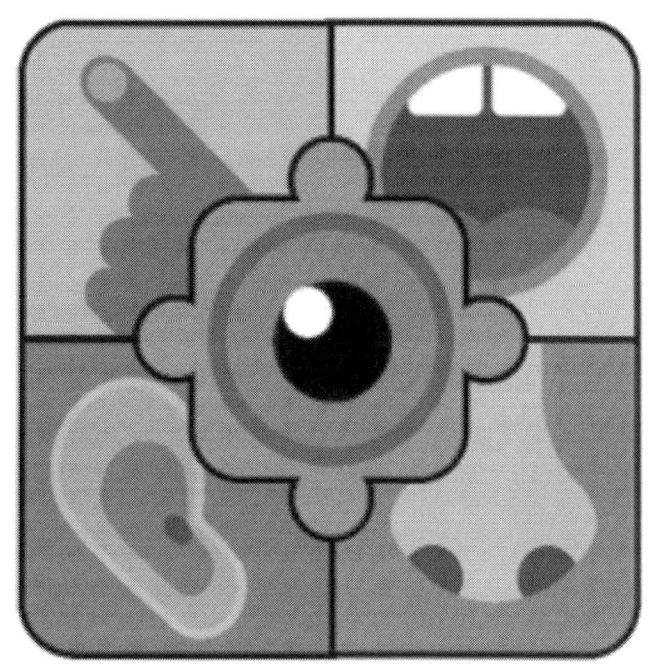

© *Tandy Ruoff / Sam Smith*

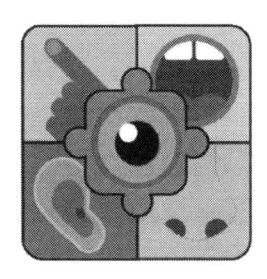

Seeing

Focus

Have children walk into the room through two rows of leaders praying for them (like a prayer tunnel). Children will feel very special and important.

"We have had a fantastic time learning about how Father God can use our sense of touch and hearing to feel His presence. Today we are going to be learning about how Father God can use our sense of sight to show us more about Him. We are also going to see how Father God sees us."

Worship

Worship is very important for many reasons. Worship will help to focus the children on Father God. Worship will bring you all onto the presence of Father God and set the tone for the morning. Of course use praise & action songs but also try to have worship songs where children can express themselves freely. If you are short of time even one song would be great.

Drama

"Mr Spuddy and seeing."

Leader: Hello everyone and Hello Mr Spuddy!

Spuddy: Hello……

Leader: Watch out Mr Spuddy, you almost walked right off the end of the stage!

Spuddy: Really I didn't see it!

Leader: Well why are you wearing sunglasses inside?

Spuddy: So I can look cool for all my friends!

Leader: Mr Spuddy who gave those sunglasses to you?

Spuddy: My friend Red Chilli. Why?

Leader: You mean Cheeky Chilli; mmm let me look at those!

Spuddy: Ok here you go. *(Spuddy hands glasses to leader)* wow its bright in here!

Leader: Mr Spuddy these have been painted black inside, you can't even see through them.

Spuddy: Well that is why they are called black-out sunglasses!

Leader: If you keep wearing those black out sunglasses you may get knocked out and then black out because you won't see where you are walking!

Spuddy: It's alright I look cool with them on and I can feel my way around or use my amazing sense of smell!

Leader: Mr Spuddy have you forgotten our scripture already! 1 Corinthian 12:21 let's read it again shall we, **So the eye can't say to the hand, "I don't need you," or in turn, the head can't say to the feet, "I don't need you." Instead, the parts of the body that people think are the weakest are the most necessary.** Or in your case the parts that annoy you or irritate you are still important – Father God made them for a reason!

Spuddy: Oh yes.

Leader:	So you can't tell your eyes you don't need them they help you to see and help you to know where you are going!
Spuddy:	I know but these glasses are so cool!
Leader:	But they stop you from seeing Mr Spuddy and that is not good. Do you know Father God wants us to look around us and to see all He has created and let Him speak to us through what we see.
Spuddy:	I can also see in my mind TV!
Leader: to	Yes you can. Your mind TV *(imagination)* is when you close your eyes and connect the Holy Spirit and He gives you pictures and movies from Father God in Heaven.
Spuddy:	I love when I can see stuff from Heaven.
Leader:	Me too, Mr Spuddy.
Spuddy:	My friend is blind, he can't see with his normal eyes but He can see wonderful pictures of Heaven on his mind TV, he tells me great stories.
Leader:	That is so amazing isn't it. Jesus healed lots of blind people in the Bible, and they could see again after Jesus commanded the blindness to go away.
Spuddy:	Can we pray for people who can't see?
Leader:	Yes we can, let's do it now!
Spuddy:	Cool!

(Allow for an opportunity to pray with children who have sight problems.)

Spuddy:	Can we teach people about how they can have mind TV? Or see with their spiritual eyes?
Leader:	We sure can let's do our Bible lesson now shall we!

Bible Teaching

> **Scripture: Galations 3:26** *(Living Bible)*
>
> For now we are all called children of God through faith in Christ Jesus.

Game option: In groups give children the words of the above verse. Each word is on a separate piece of (A4) paper and in the wrong order. Have the children try to put the verse in the right order before you read it to them!

Talk about what it must be like to be royal child…..

- Where would we live?
- Would we have bodyguards?
- How would we be treated by everyone?
- Imagine what crown and robes would be like to look at and wear

Option: You could take this further with having props and dressing children up at the front as royal children. You could have pictures up of different members of a royal family which the children will recognise.

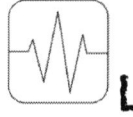

Life Application

Whose child are you?!

Whatever shapes our families are, we are always someone's child here on earth.

When we have chosen to give ourselves to Jesus we become part of Father God's family and are adopted as His children. Father God is our heavenly Father and He is the king of Heaven.

Because Father God is the King of Heaven and we are His children, that means we are Prince and Princesses, we are part of Father God's royal family!

Introduce the Narnia films and explain that the four Pevensie children were really just normal children until they went to Narnia where Aslan saw them differently. Aslan saw them as royal children and named them with new names to describe how he saw them.

(Link back to the prayer tunnel at the start of the lesson and explain that as the adults prayed for the children they saw them as royal children, they saw them as Father God sees them).

Show a film clip from Narnia where Aslan leads the four children to the thrones to crown them and speak their new names over them: Lucy the valiant, Susan the gentle etc.

Explain how Father God has given us our imaginations, (or on our mind TV's) if we shut our eyes we can we see ourselves:

- Dressed as a Prince or Princess?
- What are we wearing?
- Where are we standing?

Keep encouraging the children to to focus on Father God to receive the name He has for them, it might come as a thought, a picture or a feeling. Give two minutes for children to do this and discuss what they have seen.

"We are going to watch a film clip again and this time imagine you are one of those children and put yourself in the film and feel the joy the specialness, the awe of sitting in the throne and being crowned."

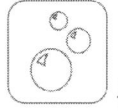

Encounter/Soaking Time

- encounter through seeing

Have the children find a space and lie down, put on worship or instrumental music. As the children settle explain that because we are Father God's children we can come into His throne room and meet with Him.

"So as you listen to the music start to use your mind TV and imagine you are walking into the throne room of Father God.

Look down at what you're wearing, you are a royal child chosen by Father God and you are very special to Him.

As you approach Father God He is so pleased to see you and now His love fills you. Father God is going to give you a name. This name describes how Father God sees you and all the different talents and gifts He has put within you. We will all have different names."

Keep encouraging the children as they soak.

After one or two songs get the children to quietly sit up and hand out their journals and pen pots. Ask them to draw or write what they heard Father God speak to them.

Heart 2 Heart

Note to teachers: *Before the lesson starts prepare a chair to look very special with coloured cloths and some shiny or sparkly material as well to make your very own throne. You can present it to the children at heart 2 heart time and treat the throne with the royal respect it needs.*

During Heart 2 Heart time have the children come to the throne one by one and ask them what the name Father God gave them is and then announce to group, "This is Princess ……. the ……"

For example; "This is Prince Andrew the brave one." Or "this is Princess Tracey the thankful one." Often children will have a name that states exactly who they are but sometimes they get a name which is opposite to how they are, they may be a very fearful child and Father God may call them the courageous one as He sees us how He has made us not how we feel.

Give room for the children to share what Father God has shown them in a small group setting. The adult can then help the children see where they can apply that to their lives and take it out to others.

Talk about each person's encounter – look at each other's pictures and share what you felt happen to you during the soaking time.

Pray

Thank you Father God that I am your son/daughter a prince/princess, I want to live the way you want me to live I want to keep coming back to you to hear and to see all you have planned for my life and to see myself how you see me.

Arts & crafts

Have cut-out people shapes on blank card. Allow the children to dress their person in their royal wardrobe. Have a variety of textured materials. Lots of 'royal' colours. Children can also decorate a crown and write their new name on it.

Prince/Princess ……………….. the ……………. one.

Games

Charades – write names of different famous characters, people or words which relate to being royal on a small piece of paper and fold then drop into a hat. Allow each child to choose a piece of paper out of the hat and then have them act it out using no words.

i.e. wearing a crown, robe, jewellery, or setting a feast, riding a horse….

© Tandy Ruoff / Sam Smith

Lesson 4

TASTE

Taste

🔍 Focus

"Father God wants each of us to encounter Him in a real and tangible way. He has given us five senses. We have learnt about touch, hearing and seeing so far and today we are learning about taste."

🎵 Worship

Worship is very important for many reasons. Worship will help to focus the children on Father God. Worship will bring you all onto the presence of Father God and set the tone for the morning. Of course use praise & action songs but also try to have worship songs where children can express themselves freely. If you are short of time, even one song would be great.

© Tandy Ruoff / Sam Smith

Drama

"Mr Spuddy and taste."

Leader: Helllllooooo everybody! Hello Mr Spuddy.

Spuddy: Hello!

Leader: What are you eating Mr Spuddy?

Spuddy: A lolly, but I don't like it, it is too sour!

Leader: Oooh that must taste odd!

Spuddy: I don't like the fact that my tongue doesn't make everything taste nice. I am going to remove it and find a tongue that makes everything taste yummy and sweet!

Leader: Really! You are annoyed with your tongue making food not taste sweet?

Spuddy: Yip, and I am going to the Potato Head shop and going to buy a new tongue, you can have my old one if you like!

Leader: Aaa no thanks!

Spuddy: Ok, when I find that new tongue you are going to wish you had one then even your vegetables will taste good, like chocolate brussel sprouts!

Leader: Hold on a second Mr Spuddy, I don't think you can buy a new tongue that just makes everything taste sweet!

Spuddy: Yes, you can and I am going to go and look!

Leader: Ok off you go we will wait here and you can back and tell us!

Spuddy: Mr Spuddy goes off and then comes back again!

Leader: How did it go?

Spuddy: The people in the shop laughed at me! They said that the tongue was made so that it could taste lots of different tastes that's why it's so unique and very expensive.

Leader: Mr Spuddy while you were gone I found the verse that we were looking at in 1 Corinthians 12:21, **So the eye can't say to the hand, "I don't need you," or in** turn, the head can't say to the feet, "I don't need you." Instead, the parts of the body that people think are the weakest are the most necessary. Or in your case the parts that annoy you or irritate you are still important – Father God made them for a reason!

Spuddy: So even though my tongue can't make everything taste sweet it's still an important part of my body because it's unique.

Leader: Exactly! And you need your tongue to eat and taste and enjoy food.

Spuddy: I can see lots of food over there. Why is there a huge table with all yummy food on?

Leader: Well, today we are learning about "taste and see that the Lord is good". So everyone is going to be tasting the food on the table and reading messages from Father God about how good He is and how good His word the Bible is.

Spuddy: Oooooh! Let's get tasting!

Leader: Yes let's hear our Bible story and then we can share in the feast!

Spuddy: Ok!

Bible Teaching

Scripture: Psalm 34:8 (NIV) "Taste and see that the Lord is good."

Scripture: Psalm 119:103 (NIV) "How sweet are your words to my taste, sweeter than honey to my mouth!"

© Tandy Ruoff / Sam Smith

Life Application

Have a table set up in the centre of the room. Make it look like a beautifully set banqueting table, have candle sticks, a gorgeous table cloth, flowers and bowls of fruit – let your imagination go wild!

Beforehand as a team ask Father God for prophetic messages to go with each plate or type of food. The messages can be beside the food item. The food doesn't have to match a Bible verse exactly.

For example: You could have different types of fruit, next to the apple you could have the scripture, Psalm 17:8 (NIV) "Keep me as the apple of your eye."

Allow the children to sit down at the table; you may need a few tables depending on the size of your group. Bring out different plates of "prophetic food". Put all the dishes onto the table.

Explain to the children that each different type of food has a message from Father God for them. Let them taste the food and see the messages from Father God. Make sure each child has access to all the different plates of food.

Have joyful instrumental or praise music playing – it is a fun party but also allow the children to have quiet moments or ponder moments where they can eat and meditate on the prophetic words from Father God.

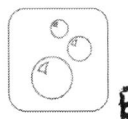

Encounter/Soaking Time

- encounter through Taste

Have the children lie down on their tummies (to prevent choking) put on worship or instrumental music, give each child a piece of honeycomb or a honey sweet ask them to suck the sweet and to ask Father God to encourage them with a scripture, verse or a word from the Bible that will be a sweet taste in their mouth.

Pray together: "Jesus I invite you to come with your Holy Spirit and to touch my life with your presence and to fill my mind with your heavenly thoughts of me. Amen."

After one or two songs get the children to quietly sit up and hand out their journals and pen pots. Ask them to draw or write what they heard Father God say to them.

HEART 2 HEART

This is where you give room for the children to share what Father God has shown them in a small group setting. The adult can then help the children see where they can apply that to their lives and take it out to others.

Talk about each person's encounter – look at each other's pictures and share what you felt happen to you during the soaking time.

Note to teachers: Children may well taste other things besides honey or sugar, encourage children to go back to Father God to ask Him why He gave them that taste and does Father God have anything else to tell them.

Pray

"Thank you Father God that you love to fill our lives with good things and our mouths with praise. Thank you that I can taste and see that you are good by reading your Bible and getting to know you more by soaking in your presence."

Arts & Crafts

Give each child a cut out of a big honey pot, have Bible verses scattered all over the table telling the children of how wonderful Father God is. Allow the children to copy words, scripture, or draw pictures in their honey pots of the goodness of Father God. They can even write a testimony of how good Father God is to them.

Games

Taste pots – This game could be done in small groups. Have five pots of different tasting food and get one person to be blindfolded and they have to taste the food item one at a time and guess what each item is. You can allow each child to do it and whoever gets all five answers is a winner!

Or

The Cream Game –

1. Have the teams get into pairs smallest in height with the tallest.

2. Have one black bin liner per child and make holes for their heads and arms make sure their clothing is covered.

3. Ask the children to come up in pairs to the table and feed each other whippy cream blindfolded across the table.

4. The teams will race one another the team who finishes first wins.

CLEAN UP THE MESS!!

(If you have not been able to have a banqueting table set up, start the lesson with the taste pot game and allow all the children to partake.

© Tandy Ruoff / Sam Smith

Lesson 5

Smell

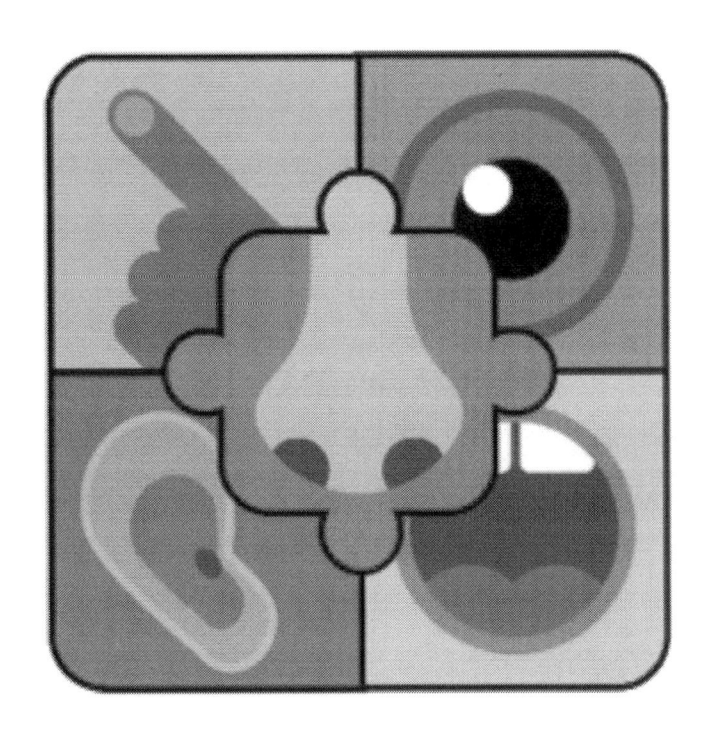

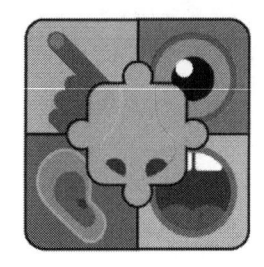

Smell

🔍 Focus

"We have had an awesome time learning about how our Father God can use our natural senses in a supernatural way. We have learnt about touch, hearing, seeing and tasting. Today we will learn about smelling."

🎵 Worship

Worship is very important for many reasons. Worship will help to focus the children on Father God. Worship will bring you all onto the presence of Father God and set the tone for the morning. Of course use praise & action songs but also try to have worship songs where children can express themselves freely. If you are short of time even one song would be great.

Drama

"Mr Spuddy and Smelling."

Leader: Good day everyone! Hello Mr Spuddy!

Spuddy: Aaaah my nose is blocked!

Leader: Oh dear I am sorry to hear that!

Spuddy: Can you check in my bottom pocket and see if I have another nose in there?

Leader: Hold on a second, turn around!

Spuddy: It might be in the left hand corner!

Leader: No, sorry I can't see it!

Spuddy: Ooooh I can't breathe, I am popping my nose off for today I can't be bothered to smell today.

Leader: Mr Spuddy, have you tried blowing your nose? That often clears my nose and then I can breathe again fine.

Spuddy: I don't like blowing my nose, my mum always squeezes my nose so tight when she tries to make me blow it and it hurts. I just won't have a nose anymore.

Leader: Oh Mr Spuddy have you forgotten our verse already? Let's read it shall we, 1 Corinthians 12:21 **So the eye can't say to the hand, "I don't need you," or in turn, the head can't say to the feet, "I don't need you." Instead, the parts of the body that people think are the weakest are the most necessary.** Or in your case the parts that annoy you or irritate you are still important – Father God made them for a reason!

Spuddy: I do remember the verse thank you for reminding me but I don't really need a nose, look it's not a necessary part of my face!

Leader: Did you know that if your nose is blocked or "popped off" you can't taste really well?

Spuddy: Oh really? Then I wouldn't have had a good time at the feast tasting all that yummy food!!

Leader: Exactly! Even though you may think your nose is not important or not a necessary part of your body, it really is.

Spuddy: Ok let me pop it back on!

Leader: And let me help you have a good blow!

Spuddy: Ok *(Mr Spuddy blows his nose!)*

Leader: How does that feel?

Spuddy: Great I can smell a beautiful smell in this room. It smells like roses and perfume!

Leader: It does doesn't it! Do you know that our prayers are like perfume to Father God, or sweet smelling incense?

Spuddy: Wow, that is so cool so Father God enjoys the sense of smell too!

Leader: Yes He does. That is why He created us with a sense of smell.

Spuddy: And so when I pray my prayers are like a sweet smell to Father God.

Leader: Yes they are, shall we look at the Bible story today and learn about how we can experience Father God through our sense of smell.

Spuddy: Yes let's do it!

Our body is a where Father God's Holy Spirit lives. The Holy Spirit can take our senses and use them to glorify, praise, and bless Father God. They can be used by Him in a supernatural way to help us pray.

Bible Teaching

Scripture: Psalm 141:2 (GWT) "Let my prayer be accepted as sweet-smelling incense in your presence."

Draw a heart in the centre of two white t-shirts - one needs to look grubby and dirty (but not smelly) and the other clean. Ask the children which will smell better! Have a child come up and smell the shirts which one smells better (there shouldn't be a difference!)

When you pray to Father God it doesn't matter what you look like on the outside, or how people think you are, it's what your heart is like on the inside. You don't have to be spotless to talk to Father God. You just need to have a heart that wants to talk to Him and that knows talking to Father God is so special.

A story which can be told or acted out here is the story of the lost son who lived with pigs - came home smelly but Father saw his heart and loved him anyway.

Life Application

What does the scripture mean when it talks about the word incense? …It is a fragrance, aroma, perfume, spice.

When we choose to spend time with Father God, listening to Him, talking to Him, it is like a sweet smell to Father God, an aroma or perfume to Him. Father God can then talk back to us with smells.

Just like if you see a of plate of food - it may look good, but if you smell it your brain sends signals to your mouth and you want to eat it. So smell activates other senses or you can say smell helps other senses work better.

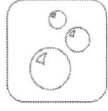

Encounter/Soaking Time

- encounter through smell

Have the children find a space and lie down, put on worship or instrumental music and encourage the children to smell what:

- Heaven smells like

- Our prayers smell like to Father God.

Pray together: "Holy Spirit come and touch my life with your presence, let me smell Heaven in a new way. Amen."

After one or two songs get the children to quietly sit up and hand out their journals and pen pots. Ask them to draw or write how they felt when they smelt Heaven. They may want to write a prayer to Father God telling Him how good He is and that prayer may be a sweet smell to Father God.

Or

Tell the children Father God is going to show them a picture for someone else here and then Father God will show you the smell for the picture - you will even be able to really smell it as though you were there in the picture. A bit like one of those scratch and sniff books you get!

Children rest in Father God's presence then draw.

HEART 2 HEART

This is where we give room for the children to share what Father God has shown them in a small group setting. The adult can then help the children see where they can apply that to their lives and take it out to others.

Talk about each person's encounter – look at each other's pictures and share what you felt happen to you during the soaking time.

Children would have smelt a range of smells and you may even have a new smell in the room like a sweet perfume or a smell of rose petals. During one encounter time an adult and a child smelt a peppery incense smell. Father God can do amazing things during this time.

Teachers note: Again you can ask the children to go back to Father God and ask why he gave them that smell. If the children get further revelation that's great, if not, encourage children Father God has shown Himself to them through a smell which is fantastic.

Pray

"Thank you Father God for making me in such a wonderful way thank you that whenever I talk to you it is a beautiful smell to you. Thank you for my sense of smell please help me use it to remind me to keep speaking and listening to you every day. Amen."

Arts and crafts

Let the children make their own perfumes. Get rose petals and sweet smelling incense. You could go on a nature walk and collect different petals or plants to make your perfume. The children can place the petals in a disposable cup, add some water and mash the petals to release the scent.

Once all the children have made their perfume allow them to have a prayer card. Encourage them to write a prayer or poem to Father God and then put their perfume onto the card and then put it in a letter box marked messages for Heaven.

Games

Have the children divide into different teams. Have a leader stand on the opposite side of the room with pots of different food which give off good scents which the children would recognise. (*You can use about ten smells, like onion, toothpaste, peanut butter and cinnamon*). They must not be able to see the food but only to smell it. (*We have used takeaway coffee cups which have lids on and put different types of food into each cup, the child can smell the food through the cup lid but they won't be able to see the contents*).

Each child will have a turn to come up and smell one item. Each item can be numbered so that every smell is smelt and every child gets at least one turn to smell one of the items.

It can be done in race format - whichever team can guess all ten smells first wins. A child will run up smell the item then run back and tell the team, they will write down the answer and then the next child will go until all ten smells have been smelt.

© Tandy Ruoff / Sam Smith

Testimonies

One of the first testimonies we had was after the lesson on touch. We had the children draw how they felt when they were touched by Jesus. One three year old little girl drew a picture of a fish in water. We asked the little girl to tell us about her picture she couldn't really explain to us more than that's what she felt like when Jesus touched her; a fish in water. I later showed her mother the picture and she was very touched. She explained that her daughter had a condition that was basically like having eczema on the inside of your body. The little girl was often unwell and would cry sometimes all day as she was in so much discomfort. The only time the little girl was truly content was when she was in the bath and in water. Her drawing of the fish in water was symbolic of how she felt when Jesus touched her…. She felt happy!

I love this testimony because as adults we try make logical sense of a picture and think, perhaps she is only three so she doesn't understand. But the truth is Jesus touched her in a powerful way and gave her the same experience she would have had while she was bathing! Wow, our Father God is amazing!

A great "smell" testimony happened when we were at a weekend away and had just finished the sense of smell. A leader had smelt a particular smell during the soaking time but couldn't identify the smell. He asked the children if anyone else had smelt anything while they were soaking. One child came up and said he had smelt a peppery smell and the adult leader confirmed that was what the smell had smelt like, a peppery incense. It really encouraged the children that their prayers were like incense.

After a church weekend away I got an email from a mother thanking me for teaching her son the importance of soaking and being still and listening to Father God. This is what she said in her letter: *"When we returned home the following day he said to me at bed time, "mum let me kiss you now so that I can spend time soaking with God."* (WOW Praise the Lord!) *Since then we have soaked together twice and he truly understands that to hear God we must really clear and still our minds. I truly believe that he is listening to God in a new way now."*

During our holiday clubs we have had wonderful testimonies shared with us by the children and their parents:

A little girl said Father God called her His Princess. She said how she saw a hill full of sparkles and diamonds and that was Father God, then she saw herself dressed in a crown and beautiful dress. She received God's love and acceptance that day in a special way.

One boy said God called him *"the strong one"* and Father God gave him a sword to hold.

Another child wrote all over her journal page in big letters *"I saw God."*

A child in the smelling lesson drew themselves surrounded by red hearts and and they said they smelt red roses.

"Charlotte enjoyed learning from Tandy and Sam to hear Father God with her senses. She is quite a shy and quiet girl and sometimes easily worried. However, when she listened to Father God, he called her Charlotte the Brave! She hadn't naturally thought of herself as brave, but discovering what Father God thought of her changed her perspective on what being brave means in God's kingdom!"

Questions and Answers

At this point your mind may well be buzzing with questions and so here are a few frequently asked ones that we have answered to help you.

Is there enough in each session to keep the children busy and hold their attention?

We have found there is more than enough. If you have a very busy group of children you may want to add more activities, but keep space for them to have time with Father God. This part can take much longer than you would anticipate. By the time the children have settled, spent time with Father God, then afterwards you have handed out journals and pens and had heart to heart time, it can all take up to at least twenty minutes.

How long does each session take?

This is really up to you. You can expand it very easily with worship and testimonies at the end. Or you can shorten – but please leave room for children to meet with Father God. Usually a complete lesson takes one hour.

What ages is the material suitable for?

We suggest the best age is five to eleven year olds, but we have seen children as young as three and as old as thirteen engage with the programme.

If I change the programme format around does it matter?

No, but as you can see the teaching, games and craft all lead to an encounter time, so take that into consideration. Also make sure you leave time for children to journal and Heart 2 Heart time, as this is key. Also put this part in the session where children are at their best not exhausted, hungry or frantic!

Can it work with children who are not used to church or filled with the Holy Spirit?

Yes. All children can listen and engage with this teaching. You may feel you need to add in a salvation chat at the beginning if appropriate and also a chance for children to be filled with the Holy Spirit, as you would for any teaching.

How do the children stay still to encounter God?!

Make sure children have their own space, if possible with no one in reaching distance. Encourage them to be quiet and not fiddle and set an expectation that they are going to meet with Father God. If they are having trouble with this as a group, to begin with only aim for one minute encounter time and then really encourage all the children.

If the children are struggling, take it back a step. So for instance with encountering Father God's love, ask them to draw who they love and what they like to do with that person. Then ask them how that makes them feel. Then have time encountering Father God's love.

Can it work as a holiday programme?

Yes. We have done this a few times and it works very well. Each morning you can do a different sense and expand it in all sorts of ways with crafts, worship and games.

I don't feel equipped to teach this material

As a children's worker you are providing an environment for the children to meet with Father God. I found this the most exciting and releasing teaching I have done, as Father God does all the work!

It would be great if you could use the teaching on yourself and encounter Father God within your personal prayer times. Come to it with an open expectant heart and you will be fine. Just keep your eyes on Father God.

We encourage you to take a step and Father God will do the rest.

How else can we use the drama?

The drama can be used as a story or a puppet show or any other amazingly imaginative way. Have a willing volunteer or even one of the children dress up. It is a good tool to work with the teaching and the children love it.

Can you unpack 'Heart 2 Heart' time?

Heart 2 Heart time happens after the children have had time to journal and is a chance for the children to share what Father God has shown them to others. You need an adult with each group, each group being around six to eight children. It is also a chance for the adult to help the child understand what Father God has shown them and encourage the children to pray for further clarification. Please encourage all children whatever they share. However little it is, it is precious and to be cherished.

We also have a corresponding journal that you can purchase to go through whilst using this material, or to use as a follow on resource for parents and their children.

I hope that has helped. If you have any questions or would like to connect further, please contact us direct through our Facebook page:

www.facebook.com/pages/Love-to-Listen

About Tandy and Sam

Tandy and Sam have known each other for about 12 years. Through that time of having young families they have grown in friendship and have both been following what God has for each of their lives. Sam in teaching and leading children's work within the local church and Tandy in her prophetic and prayer ministry. Then a few years ago, God gave them an opportunity to minister together leading the children's work at a houseparty. It was a "God moment" as He pulled together their strengths and birthed a vision, which has resulted in this first book.

Tandy and Sam have worked together many times since and Father God is continuing to impart His vision for future teaching resources through them both.

The name Love to Listen comes with a double meaning, we want children to know that Father God loves to listen to them and hear them express their hearts to Him. Secondly, children need to learn that Father God loves us to listen to Him as He has amazing things to tell us. As we quieten ourselves and listen to Him, we will learn incredible truth about how much He loves us and all He has planned for our lives. We chose Love to Listen as the names Tandy means "love" and Sam means "to listen".

TANDY RUOFF:

"Tandy is not only talented at children's ministry, she is gifted with it, this is plainly seen by the way that children are drawn to her. Tandy has a patient and calm attitude to children of all ages and her lessons are always filled with fun and learning; you can see that each child has met with Jesus when they leave her classes. I have known Tandy for over ten years and seen her not only within ministry settings but also mothering her four children, she is a woman of wisdom on all things appertaining to children and a great sounding board for me! She has a strong personal connection to God and from that place she is able to lead those around her into a deeper understanding of the Godhead. Her work with Bethel Sozo has added to her understanding of how to release people into freedom and understanding of who they are in Christ and this is clearly reflected in this amazing manual."

Philippa-Jo Dobson
Author of Pregnancy in His Presence

SAM SMITH:

"I have known Sam Smith and her family for many years, even before they became members of Kings Church Horsham. Sam and her husband Simon are an outstanding mature Christian couple who continue to serve pastorally as Connect Group leaders meeting all the demands that role entails with faith, compassion and wisdom. Sam has also served as the Safeguarding Co-ordinator for our children, youth and vulnerable adults with great application. Her willingness to take on this role has come out of her heart to serve children and her personal ministry to children has been effective and fruitful helping them to encounter the Lord for themselves. I had firsthand experience of her working with children at an overseas conference and her ministry impacted whole families as well as the children. I thoroughly commend her."

Phil Playfoot
Pastor of Kings Church Horsham

Made in the USA
Charleston, SC
14 January 2016